Alexandra Esperance

3 Before 30

What I Have Learned From My Past Marriages

Foreword By:
Diane Dieujuste

Cover Design By:
David Vincent
Beyond2LensPro@gmail.com

Pearly Gates Publishing, LLC, Houston, Texas

3 Before 30:
What I Have Learned From My Past Marriages

Copyright © 2018
Alexandra Esperance

All Rights Reserved. Printed in the United States of America. No portion of this publication may be reproduced, stored in an electronic system, or transmitted in any form or by any means (electronic, mechanical, photocopy, recording, or otherwise) without written permission from the author or publisher. Brief quotations may be used in literary reviews.

ISBN 13: 978-1-947445-09-3
Library of Congress Control Number: 2018936833

Scripture references are taken from the Holy Bible and used with permission by Zondervan via Biblegateway.com.
Public Domain.

For information and bulk ordering, contact:
Pearly Gates Publishing, LLC
Angela R. Edwards, CEO
P.O. Box 62287
Houston, TX 77205
BestSeller@PearlyGatesPublishing.com

Alexandra Esperance

DEDICATION

This book is dedicated to the divorcees who have been enveloped with shame and guilt by others.
Allow this to be a reminder that your past is your past; there's nowhere else to look but to the future.
You have taken chances.
You have learned.
You have grown.

It's as simple as that!

ACKNOWLEDGEMENTS

This book could not be and would not have been possible without the One who knew me before I was in my mother's womb. The love I have for You is indescribable. Heavenly Father, I thank you for trusting me with Your wisdom and revelation. Thank You for choosing me to be bold enough to share my truths with Your people.

There are very few words that are able to express my love for the people below. My gratitude is what I can give for the countless advice, encouraging words, lessons, and tough love that all of you have given.

To my Father, Jocelyn Esperance: I appreciate you because you have shown me that it is never too late to make up for lost time. Thank you for being proud of me and not allowing my past mistakes to cover up the fact that I am still your little girl.

To my Mother, Roselia Forest: You've always stayed in my corner, no matter how tough it may have gotten between us. You remind me not to live for anyone but God. Thank you for being patient with me while I found my way. I can't wait for you to see the marriage you have always hoped for me.

To my Best Friend, my Confidant, and my Ace, David Vincent: All I can say is: WHO KNEW?!? Two years later, and I'm still in awe. Thank you for being my strength in my weakness and for loving me, even when I made it hard. My words are limited in trying to express how blessed I became when God placed you in my life. God gave me the vision, and He used you to bring it to life. You crafted this book cover beyond my own words. Thank you for constantly making sure I am aligned with God, and for pushing me to greatness.

To my Publisher and Spiritual Mother, Angela Edwards: From the bottom of my heart, I love you and thank God for you. Thank you for always being that listening ear when I'm afraid. I love your right-on-time Godly wisdom that you always seem to have to deposit in me when I need it the most. You cared and believed in me when I didn't believe in myself. May you grow in abundance in everything you do.

To my Cousin, Diane Dieujuste (A.K.A. My Secret Box): No one other than you were fit to write the Foreword for this book. You were the only one who knew most of my relationship struggles. You kept my secrets without judgment, and always wished the best for me. I couldn't have found anyone better. I pray God blesses your union, and that He remains the focal point of your growing family. Love you!

To my True Sister-in-Christ, Brandy Leo L'Esperance: The only way to describe you is "God-sent". You've cried, laughed, and got angry right alongside me during my growth in God. You always kept me in check and made sure I kept my holiness. No matter what happens in life, our bond is unbreakable. Thank you for always making yourself available for a prayer, conversation, and a getaway. Love you, Pot!

To my Wonderful Families and Friends: Distance may stop us from seeing each other daily but remember that you are all essential in my life. Thank you for being patient and allowing me to grow at my own pace.

FOREWORD

This book reveals the difficult trials and tribulations Alexandra had to go through to become the person she is today. She exposes her journey through sexual immorality, adultery, lesbianism, and witchcraft, along with the purpose of marriage, recognizing your healing, and forgiveness.

Alexandra Esperance is not only my flesh and blood; she is my first cousin, which should give you an idea of how close we are…or so I thought! Growing up, I never knew her face-to-face until I was about 17 or 18 years old. I've always heard of her and knew she was my cousin, but we had never met. Weird, right?

Being raised in a Haitian community, it seems everything you do is wrong. You are even told how to feel. Growing up, I only heard horrible things about my cousin — not because they were necessarily bad, but just because our family did not agree or approve of her lifestyle. When I first met her, I was shocked to learn she was nothing like everyone said. She was actually sweet, caring, and kind. As I got to know her more, I began to understand her and her choices. Alexandra is a brilliant soul and works hard for everything she has. She is very educated, and her personality is mind-blowing! I always felt like she had a bigger purpose to life, and I think God has shown her that through her personal life and this book.

3 Before 30 will help this generation of millennials learn how to seek within before making decisions and commitments. Alexandra walked down a tough path to find herself. Within the pages of this book, she details how she felt in and dealt with every situation. She reveals what's going on in her mind every step of the way. This book will teach others that sometimes, God doesn't come when you call, but He comes when He knows you need Him. I hope this book gives young Haitian-American adults the courage they need within their marriages and themselves.

As I read this book, it gave me chills. I could not help but think to myself, *"Wow! My cousin went through all of this, yet she is still standing?"* Alexandra gave me the courage to not only look into myself but also my marriage. She prompted me to question, "Am I content with the position God has in my life? What role does He hold in my marriage? Do I seek more spiritual meaning in my life?" They are questions many may ask themselves.

Alexandra states, *"The purpose of marriage is often misunderstood, and the preparation for it is usually diluted with the glitz and glam of wanting a wedding ceremony."* She is absolutely correct! I cannot tell you how many associates, family members, or friends I know personally who get married for all the wrong reasons: just because they want a **FABULOUS** wedding. People forget that with marriage comes hard work, communication, compromise, listening, forgiving, and (more importantly) **LOVE!**

Alexandra restores love in her life by forgiving not only herself, but others who crossed her path along the way. She learned to recognize and establish healing in her present and future life and learns to let go and let God manifest in her new life. Most people do not understand how hard that may be until they are actually in that position; however, reading this book and having empathy will help you visualize what it could be like.

Alexandra has created a guide to help Haitian women and young girls learn to speak up! Don't be a victim of molestation or domestic violence. Don't be afraid to ask God for guidance. Most certainly, make wise choices when it comes to marriage. We all make mistakes—some more than others. But guess what? This is just the beginning!

With all of that being said, the question is this: Do we have it in ourselves to do what Alexandra did? I commend her for being that brave and strong sister. We need more people like her!

Like Haitians would say: *"Chapo ba!"* I am so proud of you, Alex!

~ Diane Dieujuste ~

INTRODUCTION

Close to a year of courting, I had to muster up the courage to tell him I've been married three times. I was too afraid of his reaction. My eyes glanced everywhere except into his eyes. The fear of explaining myself to this man was real. I was hopeful that my past mistakes would not blind him from seeing who I am now. He listened intently and then caringly said, *"Okay. What have you learned from them?"* I was dumbfounded! I finally looked up into his eyes. His look was comforting. I was reminded that my past mistakes were just a tool to build the person I am today. I can still hear his words that followed: *"I am not worried about your past but I want to know the lessons you have learned from them."* I was silent, as I didn't have the answers to give. I never considered taking the time to ask God, *"What was I supposed to learn?"*

So, I decided to grab a pen and paper, along with my Bible, and ask God to show me the meaning of 'marriage'. In the midst, I also opened my eyes and ears to learn what was wrong with ME.

NOTE: When God reveals the truths behind certain situations in your life, it typically isn't pleasant.

I went in with one eye open, afraid of what God was about to show me. As I began to dig deeper for the true meaning of marriage, I knew my next time had to be righteous—not only for God's glory and His kingdom, but also for my destiny.

NOTE: Anything that you don't value becomes meaningless.

Today, I have a high esteem for marriage and recognize the importance of it in the body of Christ. I've made a concrete decision not to enter a covenant without it being God-ordained and Holy Spirit-led.

"What's wrong with her?" was probably the first question that popped into your mind after finding out I was married three times before the age of thirty. There was a time I would have easily been offended because I didn't accept that there were many things wrong with me. Besides, I have become immune to human judgmental stares, whispers, and condemnation. I have also taken notice that many people don't know the true meaning of marriage and end up marrying "whomever" just so they don't find themselves operating in the sin of 'fornication'.

Marriage is sacred. It is to be a representation of the love God has for His church (people) (Ephesians 5:25). Your marriage and the love within your marriage are supposed to represent God. I wish I could say your love should be unconditional but unfortunately, that is not the reality of the world we live in now. People are to see your marriage and be amazed! Trials, tribulations, and chaos are a part of the process to bring husband and wife closer together as they bring you both closer to God. You and your partner are to cover yourselves with the characteristics and attributes of God: mercy, forgiveness, grace, understanding, and love. We are to embody these just as God has done for us.

When God places two people together, it's for His kingdom. It is not a random selection of partners. The purpose and the God-given gifts in each of us must match in order to continue to grow His kingdom here on earth (that is a whole other topic).

While God took His time with me by opening my spirit, He allowed me to see that there's more work within myself that needed to take place before I can even think about getting married again. He took me on a journey of wholeness, forgiveness, and restoration. With each process, there was a purpose. I could not move on to the next without first understanding and grasping each. These three topics do not indicate a completion of necessary requirements to make a marriage work; neither are they an exhaustive list of requirements before stepping into a marriage. They were the three focuses God had with **ME**. I took my time to go through the process and made sure it penetrated me before I could share it with you.

I suppose I must place a disclaimer here for all the theologians, relationship coaches, ministers, and doctorate degree-holders of relationships: I hold none of those titles, but I am filled with the Holy Spirit. I can only write about what I have been through and what God has shown and taught me. This book contains what God has revealed to me through my own life experiences and the revelations that His Holy Spirit has deposited into my spirit-woman.

I pray that while you're reading, you can capture at least one thing to help your marriage become all that God intends it to be or help you better prepare before entering into holy matrimony. As always, seek God for His guidance.

These are my stories.

These are my journeys.

TABLE OF CONTENTS

DEDICATION vi

ACKNOWLEDGEMENTS vii

FOREWORD ix

INTRODUCTION xii

God and I—November 27, 2015 3

STABILITY OR NOT? Part 1 5

God and I—December 4, 2015 9

STABILITY OR NOT? Part 2 11

God and I—December 26, 2015 13

STABILITY OR NOT? Part 3 15

God and I—January 1, 2016 17

STABILITY OR NOT? Part 4 19

God and I—January 7, 2016 23

WHAT ARE YOU WILLING TO RISK FOR FINANCIAL STABILITY? Part 1 25

God and I—January 24, 2016 27

WHAT ARE YOU WILLING TO RISK FOR FINANCIAL STABILITY? Part 2 29

God and I—January 27, 2016 31

WHAT ARE YOU WILLING TO RISK FOR FINANCIAL STABILITY? Part 3 33

God and I—March 9, 2016 35

WHAT ARE YOU WILLING TO RISK FOR FINANCIAL STABILITY? Part 4 37

God and I—April 9, 2016 41

WHAT ARE YOU WILLING TO RISK FOR FINANCIAL STABILITY? Part 5 43

God and I—June 8, 2016 45

DOES APPEARANCE MATTER? Part 1 47

God and I—June 8, 2016 (continued) 51

DOES APPEARANCE MATTER? Part 2 53

God and I—June 30, 2016 55

DOES APPEARANCE MATTER? Part 3 57

God and I—July 4, 2016 59

DOES APPEARANCE MATTER? Part 4 61

God and I—September 3, 2016 67

DOES APPEARANCE MATTER? Part 5 69

God and I—May 8, 2017 73

WHOLENESS 77

RESTORATION 83

FORGIVENESS 89

'3 BEFORE 30' CONCLUSION	95
NAIL TO THE COFFIN	99
ABOUT THE AUTHOR	103
CONTACT ALEXANDRA ESPERANCE	106

Story Time!

Alexandra Esperance

God and I—November 27, 2015

While spending time with God, He allowed me to see that He always had a purpose for my life. I remember back in 2009 when I decided to give my life to Christ as an adult and get baptized. As hard as I tried to keep my faith straight and abide by the laws of God, it was not possible. I fell short. From 2009 – 2015, I was far away from God…VERY FAR…while experiencing the supernatural side of the world.

God revealed to me that back in 2009, I gained knowledge from the dark world through my experiences, and that if I didn't experience them, it would have been harder to take me to the level He wanted to take me.

God explained to me that everything He allowed me to experience was to help my faith. So, when I decided to come back to Him, He would be able to better prepare me for what He needed me to do. I believe that is why my hunger and faith grew at a very rapid pace in a very short amount of time.

During the times I was experiencing the supernatural, God's hands were upon me. This is why no harm ever came to me. This is why the evil spirits never mounted me; they were only able to visit me while I was asleep.

I am beginning to understand the revelations that the Lord has been giving me. He prepared me for this level, and I know now that He is preparing me for my next level.

> **Genesis 2:24**
> *"Therefore, a man shall leave his father and his mother and hold fast to his wife, and they shall become one flesh."*

3 Before 30

STABILITY OR NOT? Part 1

While most 18-year-olds were graduating high school and preparing themselves to enter their first year of college, I entered my 18th year on this earth with my first marriage. It wasn't the brightest idea, but I did it anyway. I needed a stable home, and he was "it".

I left home at the age of 17 to live with my boyfriend of five years. We moved from house to house (not by choice). We were worse than squatters because every time I would get comfortable in a location, it would be time to leave again. We would go days without money. Eviction notices became the norm for us. Sardines and white rice was our "gourmet" menu. Living with a man who isn't equipped to provide for you is not God's intention for anyone.

"God created Adam and gave him provisions before Eve was formed" (Genesis 2:15:23).

It would please me to say that I was introduced to my first husband by a friend or that we met at the checkout counter of a grocery store, but I wouldn't be standing in my truth. My truth is this:

I was 'passed along' to him by his cousin
who was my "sex friend".

My soon-to-be husband was an undocumented illegal alien. The only option he had was basically to marry someone who was a United States citizen in order to obtain his Green Card.

Of course, that was never said directly to me, but I was at least smart enough to know that no immigration status meant that marriage would be suggested sooner or later. It's the only reasonable explanation as to why this man wanted to take me out and be with me while clearly knowing I was in a relationship with someone else.

I must note here that he is not a bad person. He was simply seeking a relationship for his own best interest in order to remain in the United States legally. Can you really blame him? It is a survival option for most immigrants today.

I remember the first time we went out on a date. I asked him to take me to his place after the movies. I wanted to scope out the place. I wanted to know if he had a girlfriend he didn't tell me about. When I entered his apartment, I thought, *"This is better than where I am staying right now!"* I have to give him credit: He was actually smarter than he looked. I wanted to have sex with him that same night—just to seal our unspoken mutual agreement—but he wasn't willing to risk his freedom. You see, I was 17 years old at the time, and he didn't mind patiently waiting until I turned 18 (which wasn't too far away).

The few months that I spent "dating" him, I started to take ownership of his home. I started to leave things here and there. Once my 18th birthday arrived, I left my boyfriend of five years and moved in with "Mr. Illegal". He took care of me as much as he could, while barely getting paid minimum wage. I started working but I can't even tell you where I spent my money. I'm not the type who likes to shop. I wasn't paying any rent. I didn't even have a car note. All I knew was that I was using someone who was going to need me.

3 Before 30

How many times do we use God, and when He requests something from us, we decide we don't want to do it? We cry out to God when we are heartbroken or need a new house or car. We ask God to heal us, but when He wants us to be transparent enough to help heal another person, we back out of His plan.

Let's be clear: The devil needs us as well. He can't destroy someone's life if he doesn't enter someone else's mind or body. The question is: Who are we using in order to get what we want? Whose needs are you picking to fulfill God's plan...or the devil's?

Mark 10:9

"Therefore what God has joined together, let no one separate."

God and I—December 4, 2015

This week has been an emotional one—not only for me, but also for those around me. The time has allowed me to reflect on my relationship with God. I never want to lose my focus on Him.

The transformation that has been taking place in my life is all because of Him. He makes me want to become better. I can definitely say I am in fear of God. I just want to do anything and everything that is pleasing to Him.

I guess I can say I want to be righteous just like Abraham, Job, and others in the Bible…

Ephesians 4:2-3

"With all humility and gentleness, with patience, bearing with one another in love, eager to maintain the unity of the Spirit in the bond of peace."

3 Before 30

STABILITY OR NOT? Part 2

Eventually, after six months of being together, he asked me to marry him. The marriage proposal wasn't really a proposal; it was a 'rental agreement'. He said, *"I can't live with a woman without being married to her."* I replied, *"Okay. Let's get married!"*

I remember calling my mother and telling her that I was getting married. The only thing she asked me was, *"Are you sure?"* I told her, *"Yes. He's the first man who ever made me feel the way I do right now."* (It was partially the truth. He was the first man who made me feel secure and stable…but I wasn't **SURE**.)

I spent years running in and out of different men's houses. I spent years living a life around drugs, guns, and stolen cars. My heart would practically beat out of my chest every time there was a knock on the door. I was not willing to let go of a man I found who offered me something different; a calm environment, isolated, and away from the mischievous life I once lived. He was a man who although he did not have a Green Card, still got up and worked in the sun cutting grass and getting paid just so he could have enough money in his pocket and take care of home.

So, yes; feeling secure and stable overshadowed my doubts about marriage. I knew I wasn't in love with this man. I just took what I needed from him in the moment.

Moving forward, we made plans to get ready for the "big day" (I say that loosely). He bought me an outfit: a black and pink polyester skirt with a matching top…and pink shoes.

We had no marriage counseling, so we had to wait three days before we could actually get married. You would think three days would have been enough to have listened to the voice telling me not to do it, but there were also voices telling me that I would be homeless if I didn't follow through.

We married on April 23, 2004. September of that same year, we separated (no surprise there).

God speaks to everyone, no matter if you are not saved, sanctified, and filled with the Holy Spirit. You can hear His voice, but you may not be able to recognize it as HIM if you are not connected to Him.

God spoke to me in stereo. I pretended not to hear. The devil was speaking louder to me than He was because I was the devil's friend. My vision was too clouded by the worry of where I would sleep, not wanting to go back to where I was before, and not knowing what I was going to eat from day to day. So, I decided to get married to someone who made my life somewhat stable. I didn't realize that the devil kept me in his chains of worries. I didn't recognize that I was imprisoned in my own mind. All I knew was that I had to have a place to rest my head every night.

God and I—December 26, 2015

The past couple of days have been spiritually and emotionally rough for me, starting with the fact that I had a confrontation with a close friend. As well, I am struggling with keeping my marriage afloat and am trying not to let my lack of finances affect me.

The past two nights, the devil has been busy. While I am asleep, he comes to have sexual relations with me. It makes me feel unclean. When I feel unclean, I feel distanced from God's presence. I feel God won't be able to use me as He should.

After waking up loaded with a sense of discouragement, a song came into my spirit that reminded me to call on God and He will be right there. That is exactly what I did. Just like He promised, He was there comforting me and reminding me that I belong to Him. No matter what the devil tries to do to make me feel unclean, I can always ask God for forgiveness and, in that very instant, I will become pure.

God also reminded me that the devil can't do anything to me because I have too much of Him on the inside of me. That was the best thing He could've ever told me. He reminded me that I no longer belong to the devil and, as long as I seek Him, He has my back.

My body, mind, and spirit belong to God. I have no doubt about that. The enemy may try to contaminate me, but day by day, I will recognize the tricks of the enemy — which will make me gain complete power of him.

Colossians 3:14

"And over all these virtues put on love, which binds them all together in perfect unity."

STABILITY OR NOT? Part 3

I took a lot of advantages while in this marriage. It was during this marriage that I had my first lesbian experience. I had a husband and a girlfriend, but my girlfriend had more power over me than my husband. Isn't that interesting?!? The devil's power continued to multiply over me. My husband didn't say anything about my illicit relationship, but he knew. He wasn't the type to argue with me. He would rather let me do my own thing. I'm pretty sure it was just so he did not lose his opportunity to remain in the United States… As I went deeper and deeper into the relationship with my girlfriend, the less I needed him.

Oh. And while I was out having fun with my girlfriend, he was out having fun with his.

I came home earlier than expected one day and found his girlfriend on the couch in the living room. My silence was that of an unexpected shock. I walked in and made a beeline straight for the bedroom. He made no attempt to chase after me. No excuse was made by him (in actuality, I don't think I expected him to). I just remember pacing back and forth across the bedroom floor, thinking that my stability was no longer secure. Soon after my entrance, I heard the patter of their feet as they left the apartment. I tried to figure out what my next course of action was going to be as I walked out onto the balcony and watched as they headed to his car.

I decided to do what I always did when faced with a challenge or something unexpected: I left. I always ran away when times were hard. I would run away instead of facing and fixing the problem or to even learn the truth. This day, I left with nowhere to go but to my car, and that is where I slept for a few days. My girlfriend was nowhere to be found when I needed her.

The very same fear that prompted me to marry this man in the first place eventually manifested itself.

Nothing should ever be done or said with fear – unless it is pushing you towards greatness. The very thing that you are afraid of will be the thing that is produced if God is not in the midst. A marriage without God produces the fruit of the enemy. An apple can only grow from an apple tree. Therefore, no one should enter a covenant without the person who created it: GOD!

I chose to act foolishly and out of anger. I didn't have a reason to be angry at him, but I found an excuse anyway. My logic was that as long as I didn't bring any mess home, then it shouldn't be a problem. My thinking-process lacked maturity and understanding.

The same reverence you have or should have for God is the same you should have for your husband or wife.

3 Before 30

God and I—January 1, 2016

The past two days started out emotional for me. My husband left the house on Friday morning and didn't return until Sunday night. During that time, I was asking God why I have to endure staying with someone who does not make me his priority. Why do I have to stay with someone who doesn't care about the way I feel? Why do I have to stay with someone who doesn't even love me enough to spend the beginning of the year with me? If I am a child of the Living God, why am I in a situation like this?

As I sat in church service this morning, the pastor was talking about God's seed. God spoke to me and let me know that He needs me to remain in this marriage. He explained to me that this marriage is feeding my flesh and He [God] is feeding my spirit. He needs me to remain in this marriage so that the things of the flesh do not become a distraction for me. He needs my spirit to spend time with Him so that He can water my seed and it can grow.

When my flesh is hungry, my husband is right there to feed it. God also reminded me that my husband is a "work in progress" and that I must give God His time to work on him. Right now, my focus is on allowing my spirit to be fed by God so that it will continue to grow.

When my flesh and emotions try to come and control me, I run to my Father in prayer to keep them in check. Seeds must receive water to both grow and maintain growth.

Ecclesiastes 4:12

"Though one may be overpowered, two can defend themselves. A cord of three strands is not quickly broken."

STABILITY OR NOT? Part 4

I slept in my car for three days, oblivious to everyone around me. In my mind, I ran through the list of contacts I could call for help, but my pride reduced my choices to less than half of what I thought. I was too prideful to call my mother, so I decided to call the only father I knew. No, not our Heavenly "Father"; I called my stepfather (by this time, my mother and stepfather were separated).

I called and concocted a story to paint an unpleasant picture of my husband. There was no need to bother him with all the details of my wrongdoing. After all, he was a deacon in the church! He welcomed me into his home and warned me not to do anything stupid or out of anger since I battled with lack of self-control over my emotions.

Humans love to seek help from God but don't like to confess the whole truth. Although He is an All-Knowing God, there is just something about confessing the truth to Him (1 John 1:9, NKJV). Confessing gives Him permission to enter you and for Him to do great works in you. Without confessing with your tongue, you create a barricade between you and Him. He can only help as much as the barricade you place in front of Him allows.

I stayed at my stepfather's home until I was able to get a place of my own. During this time, I entered into an abusive relationship that lasted for two years. When I decided I had enough, I reached out to my husband—instead of seeking God. I figured since we never divorced, he still had an obligation to me. I considered him my safe haven…and he disowned me. His refusal to reunite with me came by way of the following excuse: "*I want to get my life together.*" The funny thing about that is I should have been thinking the same way about my own life! After many failed attempts at trying to convince him to change his mind, I finally gave up.

Although we are all God's children, He has no obligation to you if you are not willing to be obedient and follow Him. When He takes care of you despite your disobedience,
He is covering you with His mercy.

After many years of failed relationships and losing a piece of myself with each one, I began seeking something to put me back together again. I was yearning for peace and love. My body and spirit were tired. I was tired of bed-hopping and hoping that the next man would change my life for the better. I decided to give myself to God and get baptized. The struggle was real. I was trying to live the "Christian" life the best way I could—based solely on my own understanding. I figured if God was going to send me my 'Adam' or 'Boaz', it was time to finally file the paperwork to divorce my husband, which I did in February 2010.

We fail at life because we do not lean on God's understanding and wisdom (Proverbs 3:5, NKJV). As young Christians, we may have many misconceptions that lead us to invite God into our lives while having our hands up telling Him to not come in any further. Instead of giving Him complete control, we tell Him, "I got this!" As for me, I was 'talking' to several men at a time. I was EMPTY and seeking someone to fill me up. BIG MISTAKE! God is the only one who can and should fill you. By looking for someone to complete you, you're putting everything you have into that person – which means you allow that person to become your god, and you're still not whole! The Scriptures state that God can make you whole. As such, regardless if someone comes in or leaves out of your life, you are still standing! You CANNOT be in a healthy relationship if you are still finding who you are.

In an attempt to align my life with God, I got baptized; however, I still handed my heart and trust to men. I expected happiness every time a new man came into my life. Instead of waiting for God, I always took matters into my own hands. Out of my desperacy, I thought **ANY** man would do. I didn't know and understand what it actually meant to be secure and happy in and with God.

Isaiah 54:5

"For your Maker is your husband, the LORD of hosts is his name; and the Holy One of Israel is your Redeemer, the God of the whole earth he is called."

God and I—January 7, 2016

What a day! That's the only way I can describe the purging, edification, and revelation I received from God today.

For the past couple of weeks, I felt a dark cloud looming over me. From all sides, evil spirits came to tempt me. There is so much that happened in such a short time, I am both amazed and scared at the same time.

The devil was playing me like a fiddle. The enemy covered my eyes so that I could only see the imperfections of my husband. The devil started to steal my happiness and joy. He started to make me question my marriage and had me contemplating divorce.

Today, I cried out to God because the enemy tried to pull me back to where I came from. I need to be freed from these evil spirits. I did not want to lose my joy, my peace, and my happiness. I poured my heart out to God and rebuked the evil spirits. I commanded the devil move out of my way and be removed from my marriage.

As I was talking to God, the words "lack of nothing" kept coming to me. So, I found James 1:4 – "Let endurance have its perfect result and do a thorough work, so that you may be perfect and completely develop, lacking in nothing" (AMP). That means my perseverance will build my endurance, which will make me whole in my faith where I will lack nothing. Now, I attach that verse to my marriage. I have to persevere and endure in my marriage so that I can learn to be whole and lack nothing in it. I will not have to seek anything outside of my marriage.

BUT that is not ALL I was taught today. On Monday, I decided to schedule a counseling session with my pastor for Saturday—with my husband. God revealed my imperfections and showed me my intentions for the counseling session were not good. I was getting ready to crucify my husband, not realizing that I had things that were meant to be crucified as well. I cancelled the appointment for now, but when the time is right and for the right reason, I will reschedule.

We are both a work in progress. My husband accepts my imperfections and does not use them against me. I need to be patient with God and keep the faith that He will fix what needs to be fixed.

WHAT ARE YOU WILLING TO RISK FOR FINANCIAL STABILITY? Part 1

Graduating from college in my early twenties, I expected my finances to get better after walking off the stage. I was working for a Florida State agency at the time. The benefits were great, but the salary could've been better. In addition, I was battling two unnoticeable sores in the pit of my very being.

1. I wanted to have a baby. BOOM! According to society, my biological time clock was ticking. That sound of the 'TICK' followed me everywhere I went. I was alone and felt that having a baby would complete me.

2. I was working, but I struggled a lot financially. BOOM! The idea of a house with a white picket fence, children, and two incomes painted a beautiful picture for me.

I met my financially-stable, business-oriented second husband through Facebook. Yes. Through Facebook. He saw my pictures and decided to reach out to me. His appearance didn't intrigue me, but he was very persistent. He gave me more attention than the men who were down the street from me (I was having daddy issues), although he lived in Haiti. Daily phone calls almost every hour on the hour were not cheap gestures of expressed interest. He offered me money without me having to suggest it. A classic example of this is when I needed a new car, and he was willing to send me over $2,000.00 to purchase one. **WHAT?!?** Someone from Haiti wanted to send

ME money? My interest was sparked then! I was curious to find out more about this man.

3 Before 30

God and I—January 24, 2016

Today after church service, I wanted to be alone to hear from God. I wanted to clearly hear from Him to know what I should do about my marriage. I realized that it is my marriage that causes me to be so heavy. I realized that I can rebuke the spirits of depression, unhappiness, and anger from me. But what to do when your partner is not fighting to rebuke spirits from his life? In a marriage, two people have to fight the good fight to make it work!

I ended up at the park on NE 18th Avenue near the 151st cemetery while listening to my recording of Bible study from January 15th on the topic "Knowing who you are and knowing who God is." While listening and looking out on the lake, God spoke to me, just like I asked Him to. I realized that people don't respect you or value you if you don't give yourself those same things.

Today, I decided to let my husband know my value. If he doesn't recognize it, then that is okay because I know my value in God. It's time for the next dimension of my life. It's time to stop crying about the same things. It's time to focus on God and not my flesh and the things of this world.

After my visit to the park, it came to my recollection that I was at the same place where I thought about killing myself some time ago. This visit was different, as I went there to revive myself. God used the same tool that made me want to die and used it so that I can LIVE!

Ephesians 5:25

"For husbands, this means love your wives, just as Christ loved the church. He gave up his life for her."

WHAT ARE YOU WILLING TO RISK FOR FINANCIAL STABILITY? Part 2

We spent three months communicating via chats, emails, and phone calls. He made sure I was taken care of before having a chance to meet each other. We were usually talking about life. He sounded mature, well-rounded, and knew what he wanted. He stated he wanted to have a wife and children, and he was ready and financially-secure to make it happen.

In all honesty, the main attraction for me was his money.

He claimed he was in love with me and the one way he wanted to prove it to me was by…you guessed it! **MARRIAGE!** He wanted me to come to Haiti and marry him! I was hesitant at first. I knew I was not in love with this man, but yet again I found myself being selfish and simply saw someone I could benefit from. I told myself I would learn to love him. Plus, I did not want anyone else to have him. He spoke multiple languages, had never been married, and had no children. He was employed with one of the major telephone companies in the Caribbean *AND* maintained his own businesses. He owned a dry cleaner, bakery, beverage depot, and cyber café.

I fell in love with his money, status, and business sense…but **NOT** him.

How can someone want the things of another person but not love them? Doesn't that sound familiar? We want the riches of God, but don't love Him enough for His Holy Spirit to dwell in us. We don't want to be one with Him but want to cry at His feet when we need or want something. Like a little child, we raise our hands up to the sky and say, "*Gimme! Gimme!*" Once our belly is full and see a new toy to play with, we walk away.

Marriage is not to be entered into for selfish gain.
God purposefully created marriage to:

a. Represent His kingdom on earth;
b. Show how He, too, became one as an example of us becoming one with Him; and
c. Show the world what is in His kingdom.

Both spouses have to become each other's strengths in the midst of each other's weaknesses, just as God's Spirit is made perfect in our weaknesses (2 Corinthians 12:9). Marriage is to bring two people of God together and for both to use what He has placed inside of them to build His kingdom on earth.

God and I—January 27, 2016

I have so much to say but feel I'm unable to put it all into words. As I was speaking to my pastor/Spiritual Father today (as we typically do), God used him to give me a word to open my eyes and take me to a different level.

Pastor talked about the ring that Joseph received as a governor symbolizes the same ring in the Book of Revelation—the same type of ring that will be given to us during judgment when Jesus takes us as His bride. It's also the same ring the prodigal son received from his father when he returned home.

While pastor was talking, it reminded me of a dream I had a while ago when I was practicing witchcraft. The spirits always wanted to replace a ring I already wore with one of theirs. The revelation came to me that I was always a child of God and that the enemy could not purchase me, even if he wanted to. I spent five years doing witchcraft, and the spirits never possessed me—even when I wanted them to.

With this revelation and the pastor's word, I became empowered. My next question to God is: What is your purpose for me? If I am here today, there has to be a purpose! My faith has strengthened every day I chose to give God my all. Every day, I decide to put myself in the position to be used by God to b an example for Him.

I recognized that a lot of spirits covering me were not of God. Every day, I plan on rebuking them when they appear.

From this revelation alone, it is showing me how to become a better wife. I am my husband's "Eve" and should not be the one to have us kicked out of Eden. I have to let God be God and love my husband…no matter what.

WHAT ARE YOU WILLING TO RISK FOR FINANCIAL STABILITY? Part 3

The day before my 25th birthday, I flew to Haiti on a ticket paid for by him. Without anyone's knowledge, I was about to get hitched. I arrived at Haiti's airport, and this man embraced and kissed me like I was someone he met before. He was extremely confident that he met the woman of his dreams. For me, however, the feeling was quite different. After leaving the airport, we had to gather up his friend and cousin who were going to stand as our Maid of Honor and Best Man. The local courthouse was a small shack (due to the earthquake that shook the country earlier that same year).

So, there I sat in a shack with a Clerk Officiate, my soon-to-be husband, Maid of Honor, and Best Man. They were **ALL** strangers to me. I heard that voice again telling me not to do it—then that rebellious spirit kicked in. My mind was barely present as we exchanged our vows and he became my second husband.

After the ceremony, it was time for the honeymoon (at least I can say I wanted until after marriage to have sex...I guess). He took me to one of the many beautiful cities in Haiti called Mirebalais. We spent two days in a hotel. I discovered my acting talent during my honeymoon. I had to please him in the bedroom. After all, he was my husband now. In 100% truth, I was prostituting my body for money (financial stability).

Was there really a difference between the woman standing on the street corner and me? How many of us sell our soul for money or material things?

So, while others were having fun clubbing or going to the movies that weekend, I got married in secrecy. I returned home to the United States and pretended that I just went to Haiti on a weekend birthday trip.

God and I—March 9, 2016

Today has been a beautiful day with a lot of revelations given to me by God and the Holy Spirit. A lot has happened since the last journal entry. A dark cloud hovered over my marriage until God decided to take control. Today makes five days since my husband and I moved, and I am SO happy! We were taught that sometimes, your environment has to change. I believe it has changed for the better. My husband and I have been loving on each other more since February 14th. Our love has been renewed and peace has entered our space.

I have been on a new level with God. My love for and with Him have grown fonder. As I was driving home today, God revealed to me that my marriage was my test of fire. And because I have gone through the fire, I have transitioned to the next level with God.

In reading back on my journal entries, I flipped back to November 18, 2015 when God had shown me in a dream that He cannot take me to the next level without me fixing something first. Today, He revealed to me that it was my marriage that needed fixing; my relationship with my husband needed to be fixed.

While looking at my other journal entries, they refreshed my memory. God was always trying to teach me things. He was teaching me endurance, perseverance, and how to overcome temptation. I had gotten to the point of praying to God like Jesus prayed to Him, asking Him to take the cup of my suffering away. I wanted Him so bad to take the suffering cup from me, regardless if it was His will or not. BUT, like Jesus became a new Creature with a new body after His crucifixion, I, too, became a new creature with a new mind and drew closer to God.

To God be the glory! I have been renewed and made it through my test of fire.

Baptism of fire will break you but will not kill. I was broken to be made whole.

WHAT ARE YOU WILLING TO RISK FOR FINANCIAL STABILITY? Part 4

Financially, husband number two took good care of me. I was traveling every three months, as his funds were unlimited to me. However, jealousy and trying to control my every move came with this new territory. I would get phone calls practically every minute of the day. If I missed one of his calls, an explanation was required as to why I didn't answer. It didn't matter that he was in a different country; I was held accountable. I accepted those 'terms' because, as they say, *"Money talks!"* He didn't realize I had matted issues — or maybe he did notice but didn't care.

I had a void that his money was not going to fill. Despite everything he was doing for me, I was still seeking that one thing that would complete me. I was unfaithful and sought other men. I was clearly a lost soul, and my spirit wandered as a zombie. People saw me living, but I was spiritually dead.

I have to stress the importance of WHOLENESS. Even during the different stages of my journey with God, it took some time to understand why wholeness is a necessity. Wholeness is not an emotion; it is a conviction. Wholeness is not based on which emotion you wake up to every day. If I have only God in my life, I will be alright...I will be whole. It is knowing that God is the beginning and the ending of my life, and as long as He remains, everything else will be added unto me. It is in Him that I seek everything that I need and want. It is at His feet that I go, no matter what life throws at me.

My soul was lost and wandering, trying to find a home because my body was no longer habitable for it. My body had become a home for many other spirits I picked up during my dark journey, to the point I no longer knew who I was. Drugs, alcohol, or pornography are not the only things someone can be addicted to. How do I know? Because I became addicted to self-hatred and sex. The common denominator for addicts is that we are looking for that next "high"—that next "hit—because of the emptiness within us. There is a constant battle within to fill the void. An addict **MUST** win, by any means necessary.

There was a space in my life that was full of darkness, selfishness, desperation, and anger. I eventually came to know it was something 'spiritual' when my paternal great-grandmother died—the woman whom I was named after—and I began having dreams. The spiritual journey I took led me to even more destruction. My second husband would listen and interpret the dreams for me. He stated that my family's generational spirits wanted me to serve them.

This facet was my introduction to the world of witchcraft called 'Voodoo'. I took the time to learn as much about them as I could. I would attend ritual dances, offer them offerings, and communicate with the spirits.

Do you realize that the more you feed something,
the more it grows in your life?

I fed those spirits, and they became bigger than me (their vessel). With my husband by my side, I was unstoppable with each of them playing their part in my life. My husband took his time teaching me those things I was unable to learn on my own. I eventually found out I was married into a family that "religiously" practiced witchcraft. Both of my husband's grandmothers were Voodoo Priestesses and initiated others to become one as well.

It's a must to take the time to find out who you're marrying. What types of generational curses are attached to them? Ultimately, they become attached to both you and your future children. There's generational wealth *AND* curses. Which do you want to leave as a legacy for your future generations?

I was so entwined in that world, there wasn't a thing anyone could say to change my mind. It went against everything I grew up to believe, yet at the time, it made complete sense to me. There was a sense of belonging that I was seeking; I found it in that community. Each person respected whichever spirit that walked with you.

> **1 Corinthians 13:4-5**
>
> *"Love is patient, love is kind. It does not envy, it does not boast, it is not proud. It does not dishonor others, it is not self-seeking, it is not easily angered, it keeps no record of wrongs."*

God and I—April 9, 2016

This entire week has been so chaotic in my marriage! Every time I feel that it's about to change for the better, it doesn't. So many things happened, I still don't understand why. This month marks a year since my husband's arrival into the United States. I thought my life was going to change for the better. I thought I would be filled with happiness. I thought I would finally have my own man to myself so that we can begin to build a future.

HOWEVER, this marriage has drained me to the point where I can't even find the love for my husband anymore. There's so much pain, I must ask God:

Why am I going through this?
I feel unappreciated.
I feel my husband doesn't love me.
I feel used.
I feel I have no value to him.
I feel unprotected.
I feel uncared for.

What is the purpose for this storm?

Am I doing something wrong?

Is this marriage able to be rescued?

Can I survive this?

Can I survive whatever the outcome is?

I am blessed in so many areas of my life…except my marriage. I am waiting on God to say or do something in it.

WHAT ARE YOU WILLING TO RISK FOR FINANCIAL STABILITY? Part 5

I was 'legally' married to my second husband for two years. I use the term 'legally' because my spirit was not one with his. I was not his Eve; he was not my Adam. He wasn't abusive, but the path he led me onto wasn't a good one. Still, I was not at peace. In fact, at times I felt I was losing my mind. My physical body felt as if it changed into a being I didn't know. I no longer recognized myself when I looked in the mirror. Ironically, my husband was helping me in the only way he knew how. Isn't it strange that someone can be "book" or "business" smart and not "spiritually" smart?

Your husband must be connected to God in order to actually lead you. You must be able to submit to him. A man has to submit to God in order for his wife to submit to him (Ephesians 5:21-32). How can a blind person lead another blind person, except into more darkness? That's exactly what happened to me.

Our separation happened after I decided to relocate to Haiti to live with him. Yeah...as you might have suspected, **THAT** didn't go so well. I wasn't able to find a job and didn't like staying in the house all day, every day. We argued frequently and I started to resent him. I resented him because there was *STILL* something missing in my life that I was looking for him to fill, but he couldn't. I couldn't understand what I lacked. I had a car, a maid, and always had food on the table, yet I was not free (or was it my spirit-woman crying out?).

The decision you make to join with someone for material things becomes your bondage. You're controlled by it. The saying, "Everything that glitters isn't gold", is true. It's best to look into the "spirit-man" of someone, realizing the outer shell will soon pass.
You must question and have discernment.
What type of spirit is attached to that person?
Does he or she have a prayer life?
Is he or she connected to God?
Is he or she the one whom God created for you to become one with?

When I married my husband, I wasn't worried about his spirit; I just wanted to know what he was able to do for me. We finally separated when I came back to the United States and made a decision to not return to Haiti. I learned a lot from this relationship. Unfortunately, I was still lost in the dark world of witchcraft.

In March 2013, I divorced my second husband. I told myself that I would not get married again until I was in my late 30s; however, until I got to the root of my issues, it was bound to happen again…and it did.

3 Before 30

God and I—June 8, 2016

Wow! Two months since my last journal entry! How time flies! All of my questions to God from my last entry were answered. God has taken His time to mold, transform, and renew me. My mind has been freed from the enemy's system. I learned who I really am in God. I learned. I now know what love is supposed to be. I now know what love is supposed to look and feel like through God.

My marriage is dead and broken to the point of no return, and I am okay with that. I have grown to understand that as a woman of God, my husband has to be aligned with God in order to lead me. I understand that just because you ask God to fix something, it does not mean He is going to give it to you.

There was a point when I had to ask God for forgiveness because I kept complaining about my mistake and wanting Him to fix it. The decision to end my marriage came by me realizing that there are things I have yet to receive from God because I am not putting myself in the position for God to bless me. My mind had to be renewed in order for me to see the problem to analyze it for a solution. All of my actions before being in Christ and my marriage were based on my emotions; not my mind. Because of that, it caused me to be delayed, hurt, embarrassed, depressed, and broken.

My marriage is my test of fire. It gave me a chance to find out who I really am. It allowed me to depend fully on God for my happiness. It allowed me to be broken and built back up differently. I have been through the fire. It burned, it hurt, and made me cry, but it did not kill me. It allowed my faith to grow deeper. It allowed the love for God to grow. It also removed some spirits out of my life.

The fire was used to cleanse me and prepare me for the next chapter of my life. The spirits of anger and sexual immorality were removed by the fire. I've also learned my marriage was used to mold me into who I am in God. I've learned I can't expect people to understand, because the test of fire is between God and me.

I have come too far and too deep in God to allow anyone to jeopardize my spiritual life and relationship with God. I am excited for my future! God has shown me a glimpse of what is to come. It is brighter, and I will be walking into greatness and victory!

DOES APPEARANCE MATTER? Part 1

He was 6'2" with a muscular build, caramel skin complexion, big hands, dressed nice, and smelled good. Oh. And I had a thing for men with tattoos. Needless to say, I was infatuated by his looks. I called him 'Caramel' because it seems as if everywhere we went, women wanted a piece or would take a piece with their eyes alone. From the very first time I laid my eyes on him, he was embedded into my memory.

We met in 2010, courted in 2013, and married in 2014.

Most women would want to be the trophy wife but by this time, I was after the trophy husband. I wanted a man who others would be in awe of and surprised that I — the timid, chubby, dark clothes-wearing girl — had him. I suffered from low self-esteem, so whomever was going to be in my life at that time **HAD** to be an upgrade. Appearance was all that mattered to me.

I went toe-to-toe with a lot of outwardly demons and also the demons within me while married to my third husband. I was battling severe depression and very low self-esteem (more like *NO* self-esteem). I was looking for a man to fulfill me but instead, I dug a deeper hole within myself.

I met husband number three through a close male friend. When I saw him, my first instinct was to just have him as a sex friend (sex was my 'drug'). I would frequently imagine his body on top of mine. Realistically, I knew it would be for just a moment, but that didn't quench my desire. He initially declined my aggressive pursuit, all the while claiming he wanted something more serious than just a sex-buddy. I rolled my eyes and said, *"Yeah, right!"*

Being mindful that I was battling low self-esteem, it should be no surprise that I told myself I was not going to play the fool. Why would someone like him want to be with someone like me anyway? After playing hide-and-seek for a few years, I decided to give in to what I thought I should have, instead of what I was supposed to have.

"Should" is your expectation and purpose for your life. "Suppose" is the expectation and purpose of God for your life. God gives you what you are supposed to have. There has to be a purpose and a plan for His name to be glorified. God's plans are NEVER in vain.

The third time's a charm…or so I thought.

We spent our first year of marriage living apart because yet again, I decided to choose someone who lived a long distance away. During the first year, I spent so much of my time, money, energy in traveling, and trying to maintain the relationship, I didn't immediately realize I was struggling from the beginning.

I did, however, make note of a difference between my second and third husband: My second husband was always happy to see me each time I flew out to see and spend time with him, but for some reason, my third was not at all what I expected. The relationship was very one-sided. I put in the work while he reaped the benefits. I started to feel drained, not only from my pocket but my spirit as well. I was still determined to make it work, though!

What I was feeling on the inside is what manifested through my husband. I didn't love myself, so he couldn't love me. Truth be told, I didn't give him a template on how and why to love me. I didn't like to spend time with myself, so in response, he didn't like to spend time with me. I didn't know how to say *"I love you"* to myself, and he felt uncomfortable saying it to me. Every time I looked at him, I saw a reflection of what was missing within me. It was a constant pain looking into his eyes and not being able to find what I was seeking.

> 1 Corinthians 16:14
>
> "Do everything in love."

God and I—June 8, 2016 (continued)

I took a nap today. While asleep, God spoke to and encouraged me. God noticed I am standing across from my Red Sea, and I am worried. He spoke to me and reminded me that He brought me too far to abandon me. He told me I have nothing to worry about because He is with me. He will part my Red Sea and take me to the Promised Land, just as He did for the Israelites.

I am blessed, favored, and loved by God.

I don't know why He does it; He just does.

Psalm 143:8

"Let the morning bring me word of your unfailing love, for I have put my trust in you. Show me the way I should go, for to you I entrust my life."

3 Before 30

DOES APPEARANCE MATTER? Part 2

Going into our second year of marriage, my husband was granted access to the United States in order to reside with me. Naively, I thought because we were going to be next to each other, everything would work out as it should.

This is where the deception, anger, and lies began.

Simply put, I didn't have a husband: I had a roommate. He treated our sex life as if it was a medication to sedate me. It was only given to me when I acted out of control. He used sex to 'tame' me. With each dose, it worked…until it wore off.

Our home became hell on earth, with both of us possessed by demons. Can you imagine being in a constant battle with someone who was your husband? It was like sleeping with the enemy! Our home was always tense and engulfed in anger. I forgot what cuddling felt like. My flesh yearned to be touched. A kiss was for 'show' because it was only given when we were in the presence of others. Each night, I found myself hugging my side of the bed, creating a puddle with my tears and prayers. I couldn't understand how someone I made so many sacrifices for was the one hurting me the most.

We are always forewarned that the first few years of marriage are expected to come with struggles, but mine were far worse than I had ever imagined. I hoped for the best but was getting the worst.

Looking back on my wedding day, we got into a physical altercation. I stayed for the ride rather than leave because I thought it was just an isolated incident. No, there was no honeymoon stage. It was all downhill from there. What did I expect from a trophy husband? He was emotionless (at least with me); beautiful and shiny on the outside, but a hollow shell on the inside. I wanted to carry my trophy, but he did not want to be carried. My caramel candy did not taste sweet to me, but he was sure tasty to others!

God and I—June 30, 2016

Each day, I am getting closer to who I am and to whom God created me to be. The process has not been easy. I have been crying since Saturday for a lot of reasons, to include the fact that I've come to realize my marriage is ending. Other times, it's realizing that God called me to be set apart. Now, God is opening a vault in my life that I thought was closed and buried.

For one reason or another, God is bringing back old memories and old feelings of my childhood and past experiences. I had a dream just last week and didn't understand the meaning until Saturday. God is taking me higher—to another level. When I get to that level, I may get scared and feel like I can't breathe. He also showed me that I was made for that level, so there's no need for me to panic.

For whatever the reason, God loves me. He is taking me somewhere and as long as God is taking me, I will go. I can't wait for the next dimension of my life. It's going to be full of power, prosperity, joy, happiness, and wholeness. I am no longer worried about what some may say about me; I am only concerned with what GOD says about me.

1 Peter 4:8

"Above all, love each other deeply, because love covers over a multitude of sins."

DOES APPEARANCE MATTER? Part 3

After a little over a year, I was drowning without a life jacket in the darkness and in my tears. I woke up every day wanting to die. I even envisioned myself hitting a light pole at a high rate of speed as I made my way to work because I knew the pain would have subsided (if I didn't die). What else did I have to live for? The same tears falling from my eyes must have been what kept me alive because I grew to detest the basic necessities of life: eating and drinking.

I was ready for the nail to be placed into my coffin. My so-called 'spirits' could no longer help me. I began taking Percocet pills as if they were candy to numb me. When the numbness wore off and it was time to take another, the pain of it all brought me back to my reality. My married life became something for me to endure, as it lacked everything required in a marriage. I knew I was going down for the count, but it was ever-so-slowly.

I woke up every day with a raincloud of darkness looming. Each raindrop had a message to prove that my life was not going to get better, and I carried that cloud with me everywhere I went. I was bitter, angry, and filled with hatred, with no one to blame but myself. I was seeking fulfillment in someone who was not fulfilled himself (he had his own battles to fight). We were not able to help each other, let alone help ourselves.

I started to give up on the Voodoo religion. Within it, I was finding more confusion instead of light. My spirit-woman knew that if I didn't get rescued, I was going to be gone for good.

The memory of my first encounter with God remains vivid. I always remind myself of it every time an obstacle stares at me and makes me feel that I can't overcome. After so many rejections from my husband, I hid myself in the bathroom and cried my heart out while sitting on the floor. I thought about the ways I could just disappear and wondered: What has my life become? The pain became unbearable to me, and the only way I would feel better was to cut and release the pain through my blood.

When we, as children of God, are not willing to wait on Him, we can easily attach ourselves to someone who can make our lives miserable. Each time we stretch out our hands to be rescued, that same person can be the one to pull us back into darkness.

God and I—July 4, 2016

Today is Independence Day in the United States, but it also marks a year since I gave my life back to Christ. I will never forget that day in front of my family. Both my mother and father came and witnessed the vow I made with God. I shall not put my God to shame.

The same tool used to draw me closer to God is the same tool that God is using to take me to the next chapter of my life. The last few days were emotional, full of fear of the unknown. Just like a year ago, I look back over the past year and the transformations in the way I act, talk, and carry myself. It has been amazing! I am encouraged to continue trusting God because He has great and better things and plans for me.

John 15:12

"My command is this: Love each other as I have loved you."

DOES APPEARANCE MATTER? Part 4

I felt I had used every muscle and vein in my body to cry out the pain from inside out, looking for relief. My life was in shambles. I was no longer breathing the same air as everyone else. I surpassed the spirits and reached out to the One above all others. I cried to God, asking Him to help me. Like the true Father He is, He whispered, *"I can't help you until you come to me."* Instead of saying, *"Yes, Lord"*, I gave Him a stipulation. With tears in my eyes, I said, **"I can't come to You without my husband."**

I didn't want to let go in order to get to Him. Better yet, I didn't know I was supposed to. We all like to give God limitations and restrictions. We cry and say that we trust the plans He has for us, but we are not willing to trust Him enough to let go of the past and be present in Him.

Isn't that crazy?!? I was crying for help and in desperate need of a Savior, yet I wanted to make a deal as if my life was a game!

God will meet you where you are in order for you to draw near to Him but delaying your obedience to Him can cause you to miss out on the moment He prepared just for you.

I was worried about what people would say about me. The plan I had for myself was not to become a three-time divorcee. I didn't want people to see I had failed at marriage again. I questioned myself: What man would want to marry a woman who has been married three times? Was there anymore virtue in me?

To prove to you how damaged my mind was, I did not want to let go of this person because I did not want anyone else to have him. I wanted to get back all that I had invested in the relationship. I wanted to be the "main chick" — the one who wore the ring and the one who carried his last name.

Carrying someone's last name and wearing a ring has no value until you know who you are without that person. Marrying someone should be an addition to who you are, not a necessity to become who you are.

God loved me so much, He allowed me to come to Him while holding on to the weight of my marriage. In that instant, my spiritual life started to shift; I started having intimate conversations with God more — instead of the Voodoo spirits. The middle-man was no longer needed because from that moment on that bathroom floor, I had all the proof I needed to know I had direct access to God. I began talking to Him, asking Him to make a way for my husband to draw closer to Him. I had no clue how valuable my salvation was when I added a stipulation. God knew I was stubborn, and He was working on His plan to have me come home.

Husbands are to lead and wives are to submit, as long as he is leading you according to the will of God (Ephesians 5:22-23).

I wanted my husband to lead me…but according to my terms. My intentions were for selfish gain, and I wanted to use him to make myself feel better again.

I can humbly state God really wanted me to be a part of His kingdom. He wanted me to walk in my purpose and destiny—so much so that He was willing to do a two-for-one deal with me. After the wake for maternal grandfather, during the reception, my husband was prophesied to and told, *"Thus says the Lord: You will give your life to Christ."* My spirit was jumping with excitement and joy because no one knew I had asked God to send a prophet to speak to my husband. It was a silent prayer to God that I spoke daily, asking that we would cross paths with one. I saw that as the only way my husband's heart would soften and listen to the voice of God. We didn't attend church; neither did we ever have the desire to go. If God was able to reply back to me while sitting on the bathroom floor, I knew He was able to fulfill my request.

I recall my husband not being very receptive (or maybe he pretended not to be). I got discouraged and thought the change would never come. I gave up and prepared myself to live a dreadful life. My small glimmer of hope diminished because his reaction to the prophecy was not what I expected it to be.

One of the many things I have learned throughout the completion of this marriage journey is that God does things in His timing. I would like to take this time to encourage you: If you have prayed to God to restore your marriage and He has shown you or has spoken it to you that He will do it, do not lose hope — no matter what it looks like right now. It may look and feel like it is getting worse but hold steadfast; God does it in His own way…the least expected way. Trust me! The way that God chooses to get anything done has a greater purpose and reason behind it.

It was July 4, 2015 during my grandfather's funeral, in the presence of my maternal and paternal family, that my husband got up and gave his life to Christ. I was shocked because there was no indication that the word from the night before had penetrated his spirit. I sat in my seat for a while until I heard a voice say, *"This is what you asked for. Now, it's your turn."* I rose with pure joy and walked up to the altar with a smile on my face (I still have the video). Ever since then, my life has never been the same—literally. How and why he ended up giving his life to Christ on that day is his story to tell. I do know and believe it had something to do with my request to God. I can simply say God knew it all and did it so that **HIS** name would be glorified.

Here's where things became strange…

After we committed ourselves to God, we grew even farther apart.

I recall one night after bible study, we got into this explosive argument (honestly, I can't even remember why) in the presence of my mother. I mean, it was **UGLY**! My mom called the pastor and threatened to call the police. That's how bad it became. I started calling him the devil because I honestly couldn't believe that the person I was looking at and sharing a bed with could be so evil. It was like he was playing a game and testing the transformation that was happening in my life.

I began looking at my marriage as a prison, with my husband being the guard and God being the warden. A marriage is to be a sanctuary—the place where each should be able to be vulnerable and edified. This marriage began to feel like a punishment. I would look at the walls of my bedroom and ask God why He caged me up to live this way. I expected it to get better and began throwing scriptures in God's face. He kept replying back with, *"There's a greater purpose"* and that there were things in me that needed to be purged out. He would give me visions and teach me things, but I couldn't understand why.

What I didn't realize at the time was that God wanted to fix **ME**, not my marriage. ***BINGO!*** I began asking God to forgive me for asking (and, at times, demanding) Him to fix my husband. My focus shifted, I repented, and sought God's forgiveness for asking Him to fix a problem that I placed myself in. When I began looking at my marriage as a place of rehabilitation, God began working on the inside of me. There were some deadly spirits that had to be squeezed from me before I could get out and step into the new beginning that God had for me.

1 Corinthians 13:13

"And now these three remain: faith, hope and love. But the greatest of these is love."

God and I—September 3, 2016

I decided to go on a fast, searching for three things from God...but those things were natural. As I began the fast today, I am realizing there is more that I am requiring from God; not only in the natural, but also in the spiritual. I no longer want to be led by my flesh: I want to be led by God's Spirit. I want all areas of my life to be in alignment with God.

Being aligned with God is very important to me because I want God to always be in the midst of what I am doing. I know that if He is there, the enemy will have no power.

What I am seeking God for:

1. To be one with God so deep, that whatever I do or say is from God so that my flesh has no power.
2. Financial breakthrough. I want to have the wisdom of God to be able to manage my finances better to become the lender and not the borrower. I desire to be able to finance the work that God has called me to do. I do not want to have to worry about bills; I want to focus more on God and fulfilling His purpose.
3. To know if my partner is God-sent. I want to know if this union is ordained by God. I want Him to show my partner and me that He is in the midst of this relationship. That will give me a peace to continue and that no matter the storm, we will be able to sustain it together. If it is God's will, it will also place a comfort in me that no man will be able to break our union.

My flesh is put to rest and buried today. I am expecting God to transform my being into the incorruptible body on the third day—the last day of my fast.

3 Before 30

DOES APPEARANCE MATTER? Part 5

I planted myself in God and grew, knowing that I deserved better. The more I grew, the worse the marriage became. I cried out to God all the more. I wanted the same relationship I had with God for my husband. God revealed to me that every person's salvation is a unique and personal walk with Him. I had to allow Him to do His work with my husband (but I still prayed that the work would be done quickly).

I clung to God for dear life. I saw Him as my last source of life support. He became my shelter because I knew if I stepped out from underneath His shadow, I would have been devoured by all of those spirits that I used to serve. Everything about me started to change, from my mind, my talk, my walk, my appearance, and my environment. I was being transfigured with limited notice. My heart was still under construction, as I was still asking God to fix my marriage because I didn't want to carry the shame of failure and was worried what the church people would say. I poured out myself at the altar several times with cries like Hannah.

God spoke to me on several occasions and told me He wanted me to worry about my relationship with Him—not the relationship with my husband. While I focused on our relationship, I grew not only spiritually, but also mentally. During that time, I was delivered from sexual immorality, an adulterous spirit, and the spirit of lesbianism (just to name a few). Mary Magdalene had **NOTHING** on me! I had a natural peace and joy. I knew that I began a journey that was leading me to a fulfillment from where I was once void. I began to realize my worth and with that, my husband and I continued to grow farther apart. It took a lot of prayer, meditation, and counseling to gain strength to finally be at ease to walk away. I could no longer take the chance of looking back when God called me out of the old and into the new.

It is important to spend time with God to be able to recognize His voice, and for Him to reveal and instruct you as to what to do next and what is expected of you. You can only hear someone if you're earnestly seeking to hear.

With God revealing and speaking to me through scriptures, visions, dreams, and prophets, the time came to part ways and cross my Red Sea. It was a struggle, but it was the best decision for my destiny and purpose. I accept that my marriage was my secret hiding place in order to complete the work that He needed to do within me. I had to accept it in order to be at peace and find rest in it. It was in that season that one of the gifts inside of me was stirred up to allow one of my purposes to be birthed: the penning and publishing of my first Best-Selling book, *Diary of a Haitian Church Girl* (an autobiographical writing).

So, you may find yourself questioning: *Why not stay, since God fulfilled your request?* The answer is simple: I chose my husband. **GOD** did not choose or present him to me to take as my husband. When the person God has for you presents himself or herself, God will let you know with confirmations after confirmations. There will be *NO* doubt that he or she is the person you were created for.

3 Before 30

When God spoke to me on that bathroom floor, it was for ME to come to Him. It was I who made the request to God to bring my husband to Him in order for Him to get me. The truth remains that there was nothing in my marriage that had human love—or even Godly-love. I didn't want someone to **TRY** to love me; I wanted him to **TRULY** love me. This particular house (my marriage) wasn't built on any type of foundation…not even sand. I stand firmly knowing that this marriage was my crutch to walk to God and once I got to God and became whole, the crutch was no longer needed. The scripture says, *"Therefore, what God has joined together, let no man separate"* (Mark 10:9). I can tell you that God did not put us together, but He used my bad decision-making and turned it around for my good. It was while in this marriage that chains were broken and I placed my life back into my Creator's hands.

My emotional and spiritual prison chains were broken when it was time for me to remove myself from the marriage. It was a door waiting to be opened, but it couldn't until I had the proper key. All in all, I can say God used this marriage to purge out the poison that was killing me in order for me to have another chance at living again.

> **1 John 4:16**
> "And so we know and rely on the love God has for us. God is love. Whoever lives in love lives in God, and God in them."

God and I—May 8, 2017

Sometimes, I don't write in my journal because I don't want to have the constant reminder of my pains and wrongdoings. I've been led astray and confused with my heart hurting so bad, even my cries are not able to calm me.

I find it so hard in this moment of my life to be able to cross the bridges of shame, guilt, and forgiveness. I focused and held onto what could've been, instead of what was a slight misstep. I miscalculated and now, I'm trying to figure out how to go back.

My prayer to God is for Him to heal me and give me strength. Help me to understand, rely on, and trust in You only. Help me be in tune with Your voice so that I don't confuse it with any other voice. I have come way too far to go back to the way my life used to be.

> **Song of Solomon 8:7**
>
> *"Many waters cannot quench love; rivers cannot wash it away. If one were to give all the wealth of his house for love, it would be utterly scorned."*

Lessons Learned

Alexandra Esperance

WHOLENESS

"The state of being unbroken or undamaged."
"The state of forming a complete and harmonious whole; unity."

What does being 'whole' mean? Simple. Wholeness is healing. For some, it may be hard to understand the concept of wholeness, but both words are interchangeable. The process of wholeness is the same process of healing. Processing the healing from any situation, issues, and burdens that have occurred in life will reveal to you the deepness of your current situation or emotion.

Inside of wholeness, there are multiple benefits: healing, restoration, forgiveness, joy, and much more. Have you ever felt that there was something missing? Have you felt that you are not valuable enough to receive something or be with someone? Are you questioning your purpose in life? You may answer yes to one or all of those questions, but the answer may seem harmless to you. Your honest answers are not a problem unless you allow them to control your life. They become an issue when your whole life, mindset, and actions revolve around the lack or void you feel.

You can feel incomplete by losing a loved one, lack of money, not having a child, or a lack of belonging. The feeling of missing something or someone is not the problem; it's the power you give it or that person over your life. Incompleteness distorts your vision and comprehension. It can cause you to go after that person or thing to fill a hole that will more than likely cause it to become larger.

Healing will come knocking once you realize that you need it. Then, you have to give it permission to enter. We are not whole until we become one with God. You are one half of a complete plan. Clay cannot be formed without a potter. You will always be incomplete until you actually connect and build a relationship with your Creator. Psalm 139 beautifully expresses the depths of knowing and understanding the One who created you.

We often look to each other for completeness. The problem with that is once the other person leaves, where does that place you? If he or she is the person to complete you, then you have given the power to that person. If the person never returns, then you have no chance of being made whole. When we become one with God (as individuals), we are able to be joined together with another whole person. No matter what the outcome is with that person, you still remain whole because you are connected with our Heavenly Father.

Remember: We are to place our trust in Him. He is a God who will never forsake you.

A whole person should not attach himself or herself to an incomplete person. When that is done, the relationship becomes an unbalanced balance beam. The incomplete person will constantly draw from and drain the other. Over the course of time, the relationship becomes more of a take-take rather than a give-and-take. It tugs and pulls away from the whole person, which can deplete even the most complete person because he or she is constantly pouring into the other without being replenished.

3 Before 30

When you pour into each other, it allows the purpose and the work of God to be accomplished with ease and without unnecessary struggles. Both of you become a support for each other to fulfill the purpose that each was born to do. It is imperative to know who you are before being joined with someone. I believe that's one of the many reasons the "wait on the Lord" process for a mate is important. He has a unique process for each individual to get to know Him intimately before introducing us to the one He has for us. He definitely takes each of us through a cycle to find out who we are in Him.

I understand that life throws curveballs, and it may not be related to anything you have done. For example, an affliction may be cast upon you based on what your ancestors or parents have done in the past, and you're the one paying the cost of their debt (generational curse). There are many things in life that cause us to take a detour away from what we are destined to have and be.

You can wake up each morning and feel like a piece of you is disappearing (I've been there, done that). You're dying slowly without regard from someone. The story about the woman with the issue of blood for 12 years (Mark 5:25-34) is near and dear to my heart for several reasons. I truly believe that the issue was a generational curse, and she was determined to spend all that she had to get rid of it. How upsetting is it to be cursed because of something that someone else in the family did? To have that thing be the cause of you losing your life, bringing shame and pain must be fraught with frustration. You waste years of your life trying to figure it all out and, in the midst, you find yourself isolated.

The woman with the issue of blood had a lifeline that was leaking for **TWELVE YEARS!** Place yourself in her position: having a non-stop menstrual cycle for **TWELVE YEARS**, every single day! How physically weak she must have been, yet strong in the spirit at the same time. Can you imagine how frail her face looked and her body must have been from the lack of nutrients? She realized the only hope of healing would be to have an encounter with Jesus. With just a slight touch of Jesus' hem—not His body, but His **GARMENT**—an immediate change occurred in the life of the woman. Jesus said to her, *"Your faith has made you whole. Go in peace."* She placed her faith in hopes of an encounter she was desperately seeking. Jesus became her lifeline and gave her a new life which was covered in peace. Her encounter allowed all the shame and worry to be destroyed. Before she took any action, she positioned her mind to receive her healing from her generational sickness/curse. She broke the curse for future generations with just her faith and an encounter with her Creator. Do you see how important healing can be? It does not affect only you; it affects those around you and those to come!

Recognizing the need for healing can come at different stages in your life and is dependent upon the circumstances that caused you to be broken in the first place. A great example of this is the story of the paralyzed man who laid alongside the pool of Bethesda for 38 years (John 5:1-15). Now, scripture states that he was paralyzed and at the pool for 38 years, but never stated that he was **BORN** paralyzed. Jesus went to the marketplace where the pool was located and saw the man there. Jesus asked him if he wanted to be made whole. Instead of answering with a simple 'yes' or 'no', the man gave excuses.

One of the reasons most of us don't get to the point of healing is because we have a plethora of excuses. We get stuck in our familiar environment, surrounding ourselves with people with the same conditions mentally, physically, and/or spiritually. We stay around people who will nurture our incompleteness because that is what we are used to. We normalize our brokenness, and it becomes a hindrance and obstacle to the process of healing.

At the end of the story of the paralyzed man, he was made whole by his obedience and the fact that he did not stay in the same environment. Jesus instructed him to arise, pick up his mat, and **WALK**. Now, the man could have easily gotten up and walked around the pool (the same environment). Instead, he went into the temple (a different environment). After his second encounter with Jesus, he was told, *"You have been made whole, sin no more; lest a worse thing come unto thee"* — which allows me to believe three things about this paralyzed man:

1. He was over 38 years old;
2. Sin caused his paralysis; and
3. He was made whole when he recognized it was Jesus (Creator) who made him whole.

It is important that you grasp the encounter part in both of the aforementioned stories. No matter what life throws at you…no matter what circumstances you grew up in or where you were placed…trust and obey God. He can turn it around for you! Until you have your encounter with God, your circumstances will always seem bigger than you and will always make you feel unfulfilled.

Since we are to represent the body of Christ, let us use a body analogy to show the importance of wholeness in a marriage—with **GOD** being at the center.

Envision a husband and wife, each being a bone in a particular area of the body with God as the ligament. Ligaments connect bones together to function completely. A broken bone is limited, but a whole bone attached to another is fully functional with the ligament attached. Part of a broken bone and a complete bone trying to work together can wear out the elasticity of the ligament because it is working extra hard to provide a function of two whole bones. Once there isn't a ligament, there is nothing to keep those two bones together. Without God, your marriage becomes fragile and prone to detachment from each other.

Your encounter with God comes along with so many advantages. One advantage is always having your own personal counselor for your marriage. Who else is better to call on if not the One who gave you your husband or wife? The idea of being whole is releasing yourself from the past and looking forward to the abundance that God has just for you.

3 Before 30

RESTORATION

*The act of restoring, renewal, revival, or reestablishment.
The state or fact of being restored.*

So many things can be said about restoration. I view restoration as being renewed. In order for something to be renewed, it had to first be destroyed and then built back up. Restoration is not simply God repairing what was damaged and making it new; rather it's Him returning to you what was taken and using that 'thing' for a better purpose.

Restoration can happen in any aspect of someone's life: finances, trust, belief, faith, heartbreak, etc. For the sake of keeping the context of this book in order, let's talk about restoration of the heart. We are all afraid of being hurt, scarred, and misused (something that sucks about being human). Guard your heart, for it determines the course of your life (Proverbs 4:23). What happens when you let down your guard and your heart is broken? Heartaches come with a full range of emotions. Your immediate response to heartache is to harden your heart. You begin forming the "you against the world" mindset with a callous load of bitterness.

You enter into a relationship expecting the best, but like an unexpected slap in the face, something happens which causes the current state of your heart to be damaged. Your outlook on relationships (or life, for that matter) changes, either for the good or for the bad. One thing's for sure: You are not the same. You can rebuild your heart and become wiser **OR** you can walk around with your heart broken and be resentful.

Now, your relationship with God must come into play during your hurt. The only way to rehabilitate your heart from the pain and hurt is to ask God to 'fix it' and place your heart into His hands. Ask to be able to love and trust again. If God can cause you to go through the fire to break you in order to restore you back to the form He created you to be and do, then surely it is also possible for Him to use your misfortune to rebuild a new future for you!

Without the mending of your heart, you will become detached from the next person you enter into a relationship with (or damage your marriage). The constant thought of a past pain of a chapter that never truly ended will cause barriers and ultimately suffocate your relationship with distrust, jealousy, and envy—among a list of countless other issues.

When God is the one who is renewing your heart, He adds wisdom and guidance. He reconditions your heart so that it can be used to build up someone else. Instead of holding on to what we expect something should have been, use it as a life experience to share with someone else (much like I'm doing here). As a domestic violence survivor, I spent years holding onto anger and frustration. I directed those emotions towards people who had nothing whatsoever to do with my past pains and/or had no knowledge of my experience.

Once God reconstructed my heart from something that was silently killing me, I was able to share my testimony with others. It is through my healing that I am able to encourage and enlighten others to see how God can take despair and turn it into hope.

I'll admit: It's a scary thought not knowing what the future holds. You never know if you will get back what you have lost or get something even better. The beautiful thing about restoration with God is that you get restored to better things.

A bad relationship can destroy you to the point you may not know who you are anymore. You begin to have nagging questions that will arise, such as: Will I ever find love? Will my heart ever heal so that I can share my life with another? These questions can cloud your vision to move forward. This is where you place your trust in God and invite him to take over. Ask Him to mend your heart, to bring back your identity, and to give back what was destroyed. Once God reveals to you who you are and presents to you all that was destroyed, it is only then that you will be able to fully love someone as God loves His church.

God's love does not come with human conditions. He does not give us His love based on our behavior, a merit scale, or what 'James' or 'Judy' has done. The same should be applied to your husband or wife. Your spouse may do something that may upset you, but the love you have for him or her should not disappear. Love does not mean that you agree with everything the other says or does. It simply means the love you have will not cause you to harm or betray the other. The love will actually be the fuel needed to jointly overcome obstacles, trials, tribulations, and spiritual attacks.

Whatever baggage you are carrying around from your previous relationship should not be carried over into your new relationship. It should make you wiser and not be used to punish the person you're with. In order to give something, you must first possess it. When the hurt of your past still affects you, you are no longer the owner of your heart. You've allowed the events of the past to have control. If your heart is in bondage from the past, how can you give your heart in a marriage? If you are not able to give your heart, then what is the purpose of getting married or being joined with someone? The point is then proven: Many people do not know the real purpose of marriage and the building of their foundation usually starts on sand…sometimes **QUICK***sand*.

Wholeness allows restoration to enter. The process of restoration is to drive out all negativity and anything that is not of God. Why take the chance of entering a sacred marriage with unclean spirits? It will create a separation between you and your spouse. Your partner would be exasperated and may not want to come to you when he or she is looking for peace. You must destroy the unclean spirits of your past that would hinder your marriage's development the way that God intended it to be. How can you show the love of God through your marriage if you are still possessed by the spirit of your past life's circumstances?

In the Bible, the man at the tombs was possessed. He was no longer in control of himself (Mark 5:1-20). He lived in isolation—not by choice but because no one wanted to be around him. Typically, an unstable emotional person can cause people to not want to keep company with them. No one was able to tame the man. He even destroyed the chains that were set in place to keep him bound.

3 Before 30

Emotions of bitterness, anger, and depression are unclean spirits. Harboring them brings hatred toward yourself and those around you. As a bitter woman, it becomes hard for a man of God to love you (and vice-versa). Regardless of what he or she says or does, the callousness of your heart prevents him or her from even knocking at the door of your heart. Who would want to be around someone who is unpleasant **ALL** the time? You may try to hide your unpleasantries but eventually, they will reveal themselves (just like the demons revealed themselves to Jesus through the man in the tombs).

The possessed man in the tomb would cry in the mountains, day and night, while cutting himself with stones. This is an exact image of how people react and torture themselves when they can't let go of something that didn't go according to their plan. Wildly enough, we like to present a tough exterior and pretend we have everything under control. Meanwhile, the pain is unbearable, but the border that surrounds our heart is even worse. What we are screaming for is actually to be rescued. We're hoping someone can see the truth beyond the walls we've built. It is at that moment Jesus needs to step in. God is the only one who knows what is in our hearts and minds. God can see us for who we really are because He is the One who created us! It is only by the true power of God that complete restoration can be done. He doesn't only do it for you to receive love, but for you to give love just like Christ.

Once you open yourself up to the process of restoration, you will not be the same. People who know you will see you differently. I love the part where scripture states, *"...he was in his right mind..."* When you are in your right mind, you have peace and pure joy. The townsmen saw the man sitting clothed and in his right mind after Jesus made him new. A traumatic and fragile experience in life usually causes us to become someone we were never supposed to be. Essentially, our mind and heart are overpowered by the experiences and situations that occur in our lives. Focus your heart and mind on God so that your surroundings do not dictate how you live your life. Always keep in mind that whatever God has restored is for His name to be glorified.

FORGIVENESS

To let go.

The word 'forgiveness' provides the simplest definition but is among the list of hardest actions to take. Let me ask: If God were to do an evaluation of your heart right now, how many people would be stuck in the prison of your heart? It's easy to utter the words *"I forgive you"*, but the real process of forgiveness is much harder and requires God's help.

Forgiveness is the 'big sister' to mercy. You definitely cannot have one without the other. We, as humans (and especially as Christians), should not have a hard time with forgiving others. Christians are to exemplify Christ-like characteristics — and if you have read practically any biblical passage, you know how big He is on forgiveness. Some of the most profound healings in the scriptures weren't "complete" until Jesus stated that person's sins were forgiven.

Each unforgiveness situation you keep within yourself stops the Holy Spirit from moving in your life. You have allowed the situation to dictate your emotions, actions, and reactions. In the prison of your heart, you hinder that person from stepping forward and receiving what God has for him or her.

A majority of the time, holding on to a grudge grows into you seeking revenge and wanting harm to befall that person. Now, it may not be a physical harm, but you want to see the person suffer in (at minimum) the very same way you've been hurt. You're basically letting God know that you don't trust Him to fight your battles (see Exodus 14:14).

Forgiveness is allowing yourself to not be the victim and taking back control over how you react to someone's repetitive actions. It is not necessary for the person to ask you for forgiveness in order for you to forgive. It is also not necessary (once you have forgiven) to gloat that you have forgiven.

I am not stating forgiveness is easy; it is definitely a process. The first step is the willingness to forgive. It is necessary for your mind, spirit, and body to be open to allow forgiveness to take a seat within you. All of that can be done with the Holy Spirit. He is our Counselor, and we carry Him wherever we go. Why not use Him to help get rid of the things that harm us and stop us from growing? Ask Him for help. That is why He is the Helper!

It is unrealistic to step into a relationship and expect to never get hurt. We often have this illusion that our significant other has or should have the same thought-process as we do. This illusion can cause each person to get hurt, even if the intent was not to cause emotional or mental pain.

Why is it hard to forgive our significant other? I believe we feel as though we obtain a sense of power…but that's only to the flesh. We take the assumption of power and feel that we can hold something over someone's head to use against him or her any time we want to tear them down. In our mind, we gain power by removing the power from the one who hurt us. In reality, we actually lost power. Let me make it plain:

Your flesh makes you feel you have gained power, but you have lost power in the spirit.

Unforgiveness doesn't only affect you; it harms the other person you're holding a grudge against. For a second, imagine your spouse or partner has done something to hurt you — something you thought he or she should have known better not to do or would never do. Although your significant other has hurt you, you have no doubt in your mind that the love remains. So, now you're angry. You want him or her to work to gain back your trust and make everything better, right? How would that be possible if you're not able to forgive? When you harbor unforgiveness, everything that person does to try to make the situation better will be pointless. You don't forgive based on if the person's "good behavior" is up to your standard of 'good behavior'; you forgive because it is **GOD'S** standard.

Liken unforgiveness to a dead-end road sign. It causes the other person not to go any further than where you allow. Each time a step forward would be made, you pull out your sign. It not only stops them; it also stops you from receiving their sincere and genuine action to resolve the pain caused to you.

I had to do a lot of forgiving. I realized I couldn't get past a certain level in my life to live out my fullest potential until I forgave. I was always walking around with an invisible ball and chain, not realizing how heavy it made my spirit. I was afraid of meeting new people, all the while thinking they would do the same thing to me (which some did). The point here is to let it go. The tears that you cry while hurting waters the seed that needs to grow within you.

Do yourself a favor: Respect the process of forgiveness. Don't rush into forgiving just so you can quickly get over a hurt. I see hurt as being a natural process for growth; medicine doesn't always taste good, correct? The decision to either walk around with a grudge or to open your eyes to the lesson and move on belongs to you. Wisdom is never too far behind hurt. Forgiveness is limitless, as there is no number set in stone that tells us how many times we should forgive. We all know the scripture when Jesus told His disciple Peter that we should forgive our neighbor seventy time seven (Matthew 19:21-22). I guess practice makes perfect!

While you're seeking to forgive, the hurtful memory will come up from time to time. It is okay. Instead of allowing the memory to have control of your emotion, allow it to be a reminder of your lesson learned…then thank God for the lesson!

The ultimate example of forgiveness is Jesus Christ on the cross. Create a vivid picture in your mind as you recollect the scriptures of Jesus being humiliated, beaten, stripped naked, and nailed to a wooden cross. He was vulnerable in **EVERY** sense of the word. In this instance, instead of Him wishing harm or causing harm (which He had the power to do), He stated, *"Father, forgiven them, for they do not know what they do"* (Luke 23:34). Take some time to think about how powerful that phrase is.

We can dissect the scriptures in so many different ways for each person to gain what they need. Here, however, let's reflect on who Jesus called out to and whom His reference of forgiveness should go. The same people causing His flesh pain,

He asked God to forgive *THEM* because they don't know any better. The scripture gives you insight that some people may have no true intent of hurting you or don't even know they have hurt you because they simply do not know any better. Having this gem of revelation can help us to easily forgive when we come across certain 'little' situations.

I truly believe that while Jesus was on the cross, if He asked God to bring down fire from Heaven to earth to burn everyone who partook in His crucifixion, God would have done it without any hesitation despite what His plan was before the cry out to His Father. The beauty of it is He didn't allow His flesh to direct His love or stop the purpose for the cross. Why would you allow unforgiveness to stop the purpose of your marriage?

Let me say this: As a domestic violence survivor, forgiveness does not mean that you stay in a situation that can possibly and/or eventually lead to your death. Forgiveness will come later—after you detach yourself from the toxic situation and allow yourself healing time when you're ready to move forward in your journey. It is important to be able to identify when that time is and how to apply forgiveness. Forgiveness is for your spirit, not your flesh.

In your marriage, forgiveness should be a constant thing. Grudges build decay at the foundation of your marriage and destroy the union God has placed together. Keeping in mind that your spouse is not you and you are not your spouse will alleviate a lot of disagreements that can turn into hurtful actions and regrettable words.

Forgiveness is something you should have in your back pocket as ammunition to shoot against whatever action, word, or situation that comes to destroy your marriage.

Taking your time to seek God to help identify and reposition certain things in your life is a step that is absolutely necessary in advancing Gods kingdom through your marriage. My process of maturity and growth has allowed me to change my outlook on everything; not only my spiritual life, but also the relationship with those around me.

Marriage is not for the faint at heart. It's a journey—a process—and it's hard. It is also God's tool to imprint Himself in you and your spouse so that when others see you, they see Him. If you have been married once, twice, or maybe three times, don't let anyone shame you or have pity on you. God created a partner for you to advance His kingdom. You have done it your way; now try it God's way. I, for one, want my future marriage to look like the image God had in mind. What about yours?

'3 BEFORE 30' CONCLUSION

By now, you know that I have been married three times before the age of thirty. To some, it's amazing how I got men to marry me but to others, I'm a disgrace. I've spent years on a rollercoaster, not realizing how dangerous my actions were to my destiny. One of the many things about surrendering yourself to God is that He washes you from the inside out. He demolishes any manmade idea or notion of anything you had and opens your eyes to His.

I've made a lot of mistakes, but I am not ashamed…obviously. The only shame on someone's mistake is when they haven't learned anything from it. My walk with God has opened my eyes in different areas of my life. The purpose of marriage is often misunderstood, and the preparation for it is usually diluted with the glitz and glam of wanting a wedding ceremony. Since I am now over 30 and hopeful I will marry again, I had to do my due diligence to find out the truth behind marriage and to start the preparation for myself.

So many questions ran through my head about marriage, but God wanted me to see a reflection of me before they could be answered. I never knew the amount of baggage I was carrying until it began dragging me down. The scars from the choices I made left an impact and distorted my idea of marriage. I didn't want to get marriage again without the full understanding of how and why God wanted it to exist. I needed what God said; not what I experience nor what many says about it.

The foundation of my life was cracked. God was determined to show me that I was still dysfunctional in some areas, and the dysfunction affected how I reacted to certain things. It affected the type of men I chose, my lifestyle, and the people I was drawn to as friend. Being made whole is not just a saying; it starts in the mind and is a conviction. It is the epitome of knowing that everything is in God's hands, everything is in His perfect timing, and the plan He has for me is so much greater than what I have for myself. Since He is my Creator, then He has my life all planned out. Worrying about what I should have is not going to make my walk any better.

I have lost so many things; money, dignity, peace, respect, time, energy, etc. **BUT GOD** has a way of restoring things back even *BETTER* than before. God had to restore love in my life. He had to redefine it for me to understand that I never had it before. He took me back to where it was snatched away before I even had the change to be introduced to it. I had to understand the concept of true love in order to give it, recognize it, and receive it. I had to experience **HIS** love firsthand; not what society states 'true love' is. My mind had to be renewed and receptive to the love He set aside just for me.

It was hard to see it because I was full of resentment and anger. I allowed the mistakes I made to serve as a barricade towards people and my destiny. I needed to learn how to forgive myself, my past, those I have hurt, and the ones who hurt me. I bore deep wounds that, on the surface, seemed healed; however, when the wounds were scraped, they showed the griminess of all that was covered. Healing had to happen so that I don't infect and create wounds for my godly husband.

I am so grateful that my perception of marriage has changed. I am more cautious about entering another one more than ever before. Prayer and fasting are crucial for me to ensure my mind, body, and soul are aligned with God's instructions for my life. I have shed a lot of tears, battled with a lot of remnants of my past, and accept that my past was just a draft of my life and not the final outcome. My marriage will not be my destiny; rather, it will be a representation of God's kingdom.

Hopefully, what you have read from my experiences and processes will help you begin your journey of enlightenment—or at least do an evaluation of how you can have your marriage become the light for others.

Let's represent!

Alexandra Esperance

NAIL TO THE COFFIN

I write the following letters not seeking sympathy but seeking closure to my carnal marriages. I've spent years blaming each of you for the outcomes of my decisions. I now realize it was my lack of maturity and understanding. I allowed my broken pieces to pierce through your lives and caused deep wounds.

To My First Husband:

Despite the fact that we were joined for our own selfish reasons, I appreciate the solace of the environment you created to make me feel comfortable. Thank you for never feeding into the dysfunctional side of me.

To My Second Husband:

Believe it or not, I don't blame you for my misguided steps into the dark world. It has given me a vantage view to understand certain things better with my new walk with God. I ask you for forgiveness for taking your kindness for a weakness. I portrayed a love for you that didn't exist. Sorry for using and abusing your heart while you gave it to me on a silver platter.

To My Third Husband:

Surprisingly, I thank God for you. You were the wakeup call I needed to love myself and to get my life back on track. Although we wrestled with the idea of reconciliation, we both knew it would be a step backwards – for both of us. Sorry for always trying to be the head and not trusting you to lead. Sorry for using different fragments from my past relationships to try to make a full picture of what a husband should be. Just as I blamed you for not knowing, I blamed myself for thinking I knew it all…because I didn't. I am proud of the progress of forgiveness we have made with the help of God.

Alexandra Esperance

I have grown into a woman who understands that my beauty lies in my ashes. I should have found myself first before attaching to each of you. Since my heart has been healed, I released everything that caused a barrier to progress in life. I pray that the experience with me does not cause the demise of your next relationship — and vice-versa.

With love and respect, this is the nail to the coffin of my past marriages.

Sincerely,

The New ME

ABOUT THE AUTHOR

A Florida native born to immigrant parents from Haiti, at an early age, Alexandra understood their struggles and the importance of seeking help from a Higher Power. Well into her young adult years, she battled forces between the worlds of darkness and light.

Full of confusion with her father's belief and practice of Voodoo, along with being led by her mother to church, she struggled to find the truth and her way to the road of righteousness.

While she wavered in and out of religion, Alexandra finally had an encounter with God on her bathroom floor in her late twenties. The encounter ignited her journey with God, which blossomed into an everlasting Father-Daughter relationship. She frequently uses the term "Daddy" in prayer or in simple conversation to represent the closeness of their relationship and to show how reachable He is to those who are seeking Him.

As her love for Him grew, the love for His forgotten children grew even more. Her hidden gift of writing was unveiled with the birthing of Amazon's Best-Selling Book, *Diary of a Haitian Church Girl*, wherein she shares her experiences of growing with light and darkness. She is passionate about being the voice for the misunderstood and the underdog. Alexandra takes each pen stroke seriously because she recognizes that they have the potential to break yokes and destroy the lies that may block someone's path.

Her philanthropic work began by contributing and becoming a Co-Author of the #1 Best-Selling series, *God Says I am Battle-Scar Free*, a project that gives voices to domestic violence victors to let them know they can tear off the label of victimization and become survivors.

She decided to use the pen name Alexandra Esperance instead of her maiden name to prove to her father and ancestors that the family name will be great because of the Almighty God and nothing else. It stems from her believing God will destroy the darkness over her paternal family name to create a new beginning for future generations.

Alexandra decided to extend herself by founding "Trinity Office Solutions, LLC" — a Christian-based entity providing data entry services. She also provides consultation and training services to companies and community partners by sharing her expertise of 10 years in social services in the public assistance sector.

The next chapter of her life exemplifies the deep maturing of her relationship with her God. She's an unapologetic servant of God and is determined and willing to fulfill the purpose that God has for her life.

CONTACT ALEXANDRA ESPERANCE

 www.AlexandraEsperance.com

 AlexandraEsperance@yahoo.com

 @OfficiallyAlexandraEsperance

 @Alexandra.Esperance

 http://bit.ly/AlexandraEsperance

www.ingramcontent.com/pod-product-compliance
Lightning Source LLC
Chambersburg PA
CBHW071522080526
44588CB00011B/1533